KU-120-760

S00000902796

BRIGHT IDEA BOOKS

AMAZING Islands AROUND THE WORLD

by Pat Tanumihardja

raintree
a Capstone company — publishers for children

Raintree is an imprint of Capstone Global Library Limited, a company incorporated in England and Wales having its registered office at 264 Banbury Road, Oxford, OX2 7DY – Registered company number: 6695582

www.raintree.co.uk
myorders@raintree.co.uk

Text © Capstone Global Library Limited 2020
The moral rights of the proprietor have been asserted.

All rights reserved. No part of this publication may be reproduced in any form or by any means (including photocopying or storing it in any medium by electronic means and whether or not transiently or incidentally to some other use of this publication) without the written permission of the copyright owner, except in accordance with the provisions of the Copyright, Designs and Patents Act 1988 or under the terms of a licence issued by the Copyright Licensing Agency, Barnard's Inn, 86 Fetter Lane, London, EC4A 1EN (www.cla.co.uk). Applications for the copyright owner's written permission should be addressed to the publisher.

Edited by Claire Vanden Branden
Designed by Becky Daum
Original illustrations © Capstone Global Library Limited 2020
Production by Dan Peluso
Originated by Capstone Global Library Ltd
Printed and bound in India

ISBN 978 1 4747 7467 3 (hardback)
ISBN 978 1 4747 8120 6 (paperback)

British Library Cataloguing in Publication Data
A full catalogue record for this book is available from the British Library.

DUDLEY
LIBRARIES

S00000902796

Askews & Holts	11-Nov-2019
C551.42	£12.99
2SLS	

Acknowledgements
We would like to thank the following for permission to reproduce photographs: iStockphoto: kzubrycki, cover, Nnehring, 26–27, urosr, 14–15; Newscom: Gerry Ellis/Minden Pictures, 13; Shutterstock Images: Andrey Bayda, 17, Denis Burdin, 7, 28, Don Mammoser, 23, Muhammad Nurudin, 5, nelzajamal, 18–19, Paolo Grandi, 9, RugliG, 20–21, Sergey Uryadnikov, 24–25, underworld, 10–11, 30–31.

Every effort has been made to contact copyright holders of material reproduced in this book. Any omissions will be rectified in subsequent printings if notice is given to the publisher.

All the internet addresses (URLs) given in this book were valid at the time of going to press. However, due to the dynamic nature of the internet, some addresses may have changed, or sites may have changed or ceased to exist since publication. While the author and publisher regret any inconvenience this may cause readers, no responsibility for any such changes can be accepted by either the author or the publisher.

CONTENTS

CHAPTER ONE
AMAZING ISLANDS 4

CHAPTER TWO
GREENLAND 6

CHAPTER THREE
VOLCANIC ISLANDS 8

CHAPTER FOUR
CORAL ISLANDS............... 12

CHAPTER FIVE
COLOURFUL BEACHES 16

CHAPTER SIX
PLANTS AND ANIMALS...... 22

Glossary 28
Top islands to visit 29
Activity 30
Find out more 32
Index............................... 32

CHAPTER 1

AMAZING
Islands

Some islands are countries. Others are just small pieces of rock. An island is land that has water all around it. It takes many years for an island to form.

Most islands are in the ocean. But some are in lakes and rivers. Islands can have many amazing features. Some have beaches with colourful sand. Others are covered in ice. Discover some of the world's most amazing islands.

Tiny islands are called islets.

CHAPTER 2

GREENLAND

Greenland is the world's largest island. It is in the Atlantic Ocean and the Arctic Ocean. It has an area of 2,166,085 square kilometres (836,330 square miles). Almost all of it is covered in ice. The ice can be up to 3 kilometres (2 miles) thick.

SMALLEST ISLAND

Just Room Enough Island is near New York, USA. It is on a river and is the smallest island that people live on. There is just enough room for a house, a tree and a small beach.

Most of Greenland is cold and icy.

CHAPTER 3

VOLCANIC
Islands

The Aeolian Islands are in the Mediterranean Sea. These seven islands were made from volcanoes. They are known for their hot mud baths. Mud baths are made from hot rock warming Earth.

The Aeolian Islands are part of Italy.

9

Lanzarote is in the Atlantic Ocean. Flowing lava once covered much of the island. When the lava cooled it formed twisted and folded shapes.

Lanzarote is off the coast of Africa. But it is owned by Spain.

10

Wizard Island is in a lake in Oregon, USA. The island and lake are in the crater of a volcano. Its name comes from its shape. It looks like a wizard's hat!

Interesting animals live on the island. One of these animals is the blind **albino** crab. It can't be found anywhere else.

CHAPTER 4

CORAL
Islands

Some islands are made from **coral**. Heron Island is a coral **cay**. It is a sandy island on top of a coral **reef**. It is very small. It only takes 20 minutes to walk around the whole island. People enjoy snorkelling in the waters around the island.

Heron Island lies on top of the Great Barrier Reef in Australia.

13

Coral reefs can grow around islands. Sometimes the islands sink back underwater. The coral keeps growing above the surface and a ring of coral forms. This is called an **atoll**. The body of water inside an atoll is called a lagoon.

MANY ISLANDS

The Maldives is a country in the Indian Ocean. It has more than 1,190 islands and 26 atolls.

Rangiroa means "endless skies" in the Tahitian language.

The Rangiroa atoll is in the Pacific Ocean. It is one of the world's biggest atolls. Its lagoon is huge. It is 280 kilometres (174 miles) wide.

CHAPTER 5

COLOURFUL
Beaches

Many islands have white sandy beaches. But beaches can be other colours too.

Reynisfjara Beach is in Iceland.

This beach has black sand. It is black because of the nearby volcanoes.

The black sand is made up of volcanic ash that has broken into small pieces.

People from all over the world visit the beautiful pink sand beaches of Indonesia.

Indonesia has around 17,500 islands. Some have pink beaches. This colour comes from crushed coral and shells.

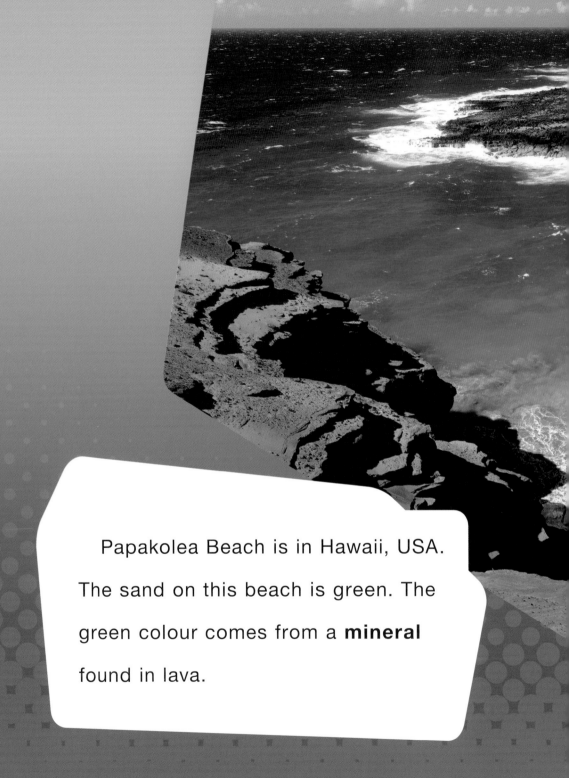

Papakolea Beach is in Hawaii, USA. The sand on this beach is green. The green colour comes from a **mineral** found in lava.

Papakolea Beach is one of only two green beaches in the world.

CHAPTER 6

PLANTS AND Animals

The Galápagos Islands are in the Pacific Ocean. Many interesting animals live on the island. Some of these animals can't be found anywhere else in the world.

The giant Galápagos tortoise is the world's largest tortoise. It can grow to be as big as a lion. It can also live to be over 150 years old.

The giant Galápagos tortoise can weigh more than 180 kilograms (400 pounds).

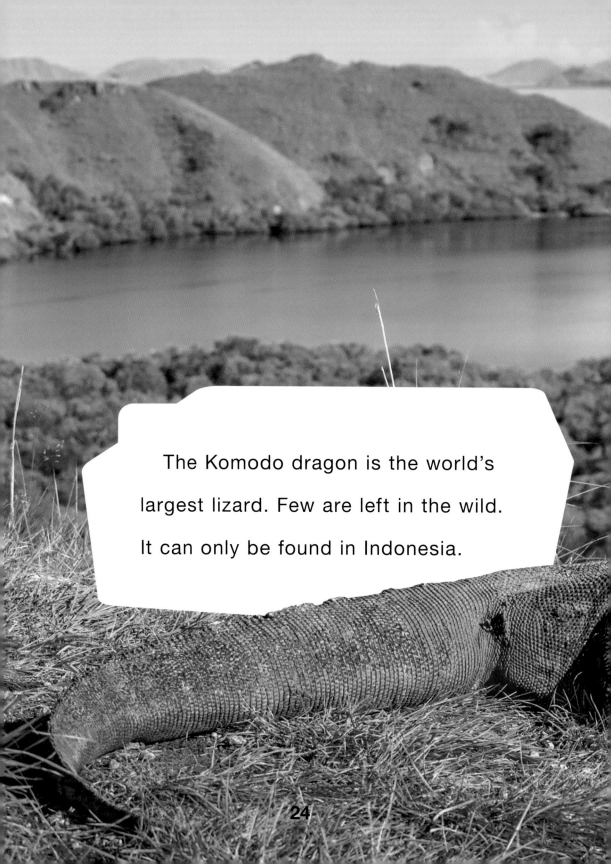

The Komodo dragon is the world's largest lizard. Few are left in the wild. It can only be found in Indonesia.

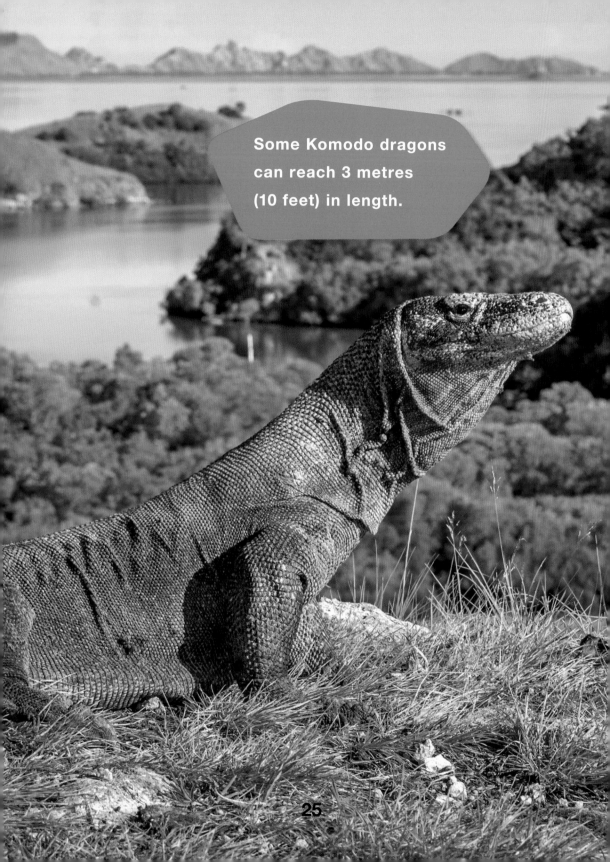

Some Komodo dragons can reach 3 metres (10 feet) in length.

Beautiful, bright flowers cover the island of Kauai.

Kauai is known as the Garden Island. It is part of Hawaii. Beautiful plants grow on the island. Clay's hibiscus is a red flower. It only grows on Kauai.

GLOSSARY

albino
person or animal without
natural colouring

atoll
ring made of coral that
surrounds a lagoon

cay
small sandy island on top of a
coral reef

coral
tiny marine animals that have
hard shells that look like rock

mineral
substance that occurs
in nature

reef
strip of rock, sand or coral
close to the surface of
an ocean

TOP ISLANDS TO VISIT

AEOLIAN ISLANDS, ITALY
Take a dip in the hot mud baths of these volcanic islands.

GALÁPAGOS ISLANDS
See the largest tortoise in the world.

GREENLAND
Visit the world's largest island.

HERON ISLAND, AUSTRALIA
Go snorkelling on this small coral island.

INDONESIA
View the pink sand beaches on one of these warm islands.

KAUAI, HAWAII, USA
See the beautiful plants on the Garden Island.

KOMODO ISLAND, INDONESIA
Take pictures of the largest lizard in the world.

LANZAROTE, SPAIN
See the interesting shapes that cooled lava has made.

PAPAKOLEA BEACH, HAWAII, USA
Take a trip to the green sand beach.

RANGIROA ATOLL, FRENCH POLYNESIA
Visit one of the world's largest atolls.

REYNISFJARA BEACH, ICELAND
Experience the black sand beach on this island.

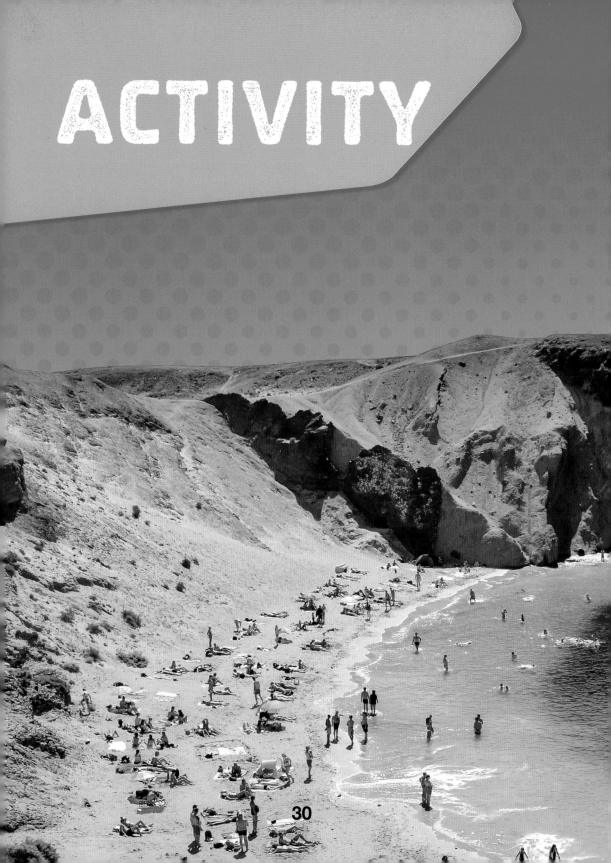

ACTIVITY

MAKE YOUR OWN ISLAND!

Make a model of an island with modelling clay or cardboard. Create your dream landscape on your island. You can include wildlife, flowers, fruit trees, sandy beaches or mountains. Use recyclable materials such as plastic bottles and boxes. Use construction paper to add colour to your island. Then show it to your friends or family.

FIND OUT MORE

Books

Islands (Learning about Landforms), Ellen Labrecque (Raintree, 2015)

Islands of the World (Engage Literacy), Kassandra Radomski (Raintree, 2017)

The World's Most Amazing Islands (Landform Top Tens), Anita Ganeri (Raintree, 2010)

Websites

www.bbc.com/bitesize/articles/zk9cxyc
Explore the Galápagos Islands!

www.dkfindout.com/uk/earth/oceans-and-seas
Find out more about oceans and seas.

INDEX

Aeolian Islands 8

Clay's hibiscus 27
coral 12, 14, 18

Galápagos Islands
     22–23
giant Galápagos
     tortoise 23
Greenland 6

Hawaii 20, 27
Heron Island 12

Iceland 17
Indonesia 18, 24

Just Room Enough
     Island 7

Kauai 27
Komodo dragon 24

Lanzarote 10–11
lava 10, 20

Maldives 14

Papakolea Beach 20

Rangiroa atoll 15
Reynisfjara Beach
     17

Wizard's Island 11